MARKETING AND MAKING SALES WITH SOCIAL MEDIA IN 2020

A STEP BY STEP GUIDE TO MAKING MASSIVE SALES ORGANICALLY (DIY)

WHATSAPP

TWITTER

FACEBOOK

INSTAGRAM

JOHN CONTON

Golden rule to learning
"Our Brains evolved to learn by doing things, not by hearing about them. This is one of the reasons that for a lot of skills, it is much better to spend about two thirds of your time testing yourself on it rather than absorbing it"
---DANIEL COYLE, 2020

For every knowledge you will acquire from this book, make sure to test it and select the one that works best for your kind of business, every business has a different revenue funnel or model; what works for A might not work for B.
Do not just read without practicing what is herein, read and practicalise. Don't stop testing your approaches.

Copyright

.

Contents

Question 2: How will you intentionally transform cold prospects into leads, sales, and more sales?

If you have a single customer, a Customer Value Journey already exists for your company. The question is whether you generated that single customer intentionally and more importantly, could you do it over and over again?

THE DELICATE ART OF SELLING

The art of selling is so multi-dimensional and is yet to be over emphasized, we can categorise it into online and offline selling; Selling is the act of engaging with prospects in a special way, that will result into exchange of values.

I don't know if I am making sense? Ok, let me explain myself further...

My sales Journey!

I remembered some couple of years back after my high school, I would volunteer to help my sister stay in her store to sell, and I was only 16 years old as at the time.

She would travel for weeks and leave me with handling of buying her stocks, making sales and keeping her money with proper record keeping, and accounted for every penny spent. I would attend to customers and smile more with them, if I don't know a price to a product, i would put a call through and persuade the customers to hold one while I confirm.

She got me my first mobile phone hehe!

Whenever she's back from her journey she would take over her shop, she would always tell me that my customers were always asking of me and most of them attest that they love my approach and would want me to sell to them again.

When it was time to enter the university, I thought of a course to apply for, I chose marketing because I knew I was good at this; but as at the time, marketing was not accredited in my institution so I optioned for insurance since I'd still be privileged to practise marketing as a course but not as a degree.

To cut the long story short, I usually pass all my marketing courses effortlessly also finish all my exams at any of my marketing course before anyone else in the class. My persuasive skills were excellent I must good.

(Little secret, don't tell anyone... my friends would even call me along to help them talk to their crush.....LOL)

What was I saying in essence? I was able to discover my selling skills through selling for my sister and now I am finding selling my skill as a product.

"You too can sell"

This world is a selling place, no matter who you are or what you do on earth, you must find ways around selling to make money; Be it an engineer that builds engines and houses to a doctor that heals, to an inventor that invent, to a singer that sings, to a mechanic that repairs, any of the these ways, you must find your way around selling your product or services,

"everybody is a marketer."

We must always come up with exceptional and creative ways of selling our product and services differently from how everybody else would sell and also execute our strategies with the mindset of a problem solver rather than being a salesman.

It is no more a speculation that the fastest way to reach larger audience in this 21st century is through social media marketing. What all businesses are aiming at is to increase their audience reach both online and offline, getting more clients and making unlimited sales

The old ways of engaging and converting customers are gradually going into extinction. An old way of reaching an audience for conversion is through the use of cold calling.

i.e. it was not so long that some companies stopped taking books to make calls to reach out to people to pitch their product.

For example, companies would get around 20 sales meetings with prospects that are willing to convert in every 1600 calls made.

Wow!

This must have taken a whole lot of time, energy and resources put into getting just 20 prospects

Anyways, let's continue....

In the past, cold calling was the only way to find new business, but in recent years social media has made it possible to make your sales right in the comfort of your room.

Finding your prospects is just a matter of searching and clicking on a few buttons and all the work is done.

Interesting right?

But do you know that, one major problem a lot of start-up business are facing is lack of experience and inconsistency. You must agree with me that as an apprentice learning a craft from your boss, you must spend a particular period of time learning the art of such craft; same process should be adopted into the art of selling online.

How do you learn this art?

If you run a small business, you will have to look at the approach being used by big organisations or brand of top competitor, how they structure their platform also you can check their comment section and there you have the exact consumer of your product.

I know you are wondering why you have to learn from them but truth be told, you just need a mentor and they could be the mentor you need; these people spend fortune in piloting their brand. Learn their approach, use their approach.

It's time to say hi and try to connect with the audience on your mentor's page; personalize a message targeting the audience. Design a sales magnet content to always call them by their name, this way they develop this feeling of being known personally.

So try to be briefer and more specific, this is not the time to speak heavy grammar. Below are examples of the kind of message to send to new prospects.

Feel free to use these templates and you can also tweak the message as you like, but when you get your first deal remember me in your paradise...Lol

For big businesses (B2B) you can do something like this;

-Hello [first name]. I see you work at [their company name]. I have been following your work for a while now; you are doing an amazing job! I would love to hear more about your story and success. Looking forward to connecting with you

- Hello [first name]. I see you work at [their company name]. It looks like we have a mutual interest in [mutual connection name] would you like to connect?

-HI [first name], I have joined [group name] on [social media platform] and I have really enjoyed reading from you, are you willing to connect with me?

For small businesses B2C (SME) trying to connect with their prospects [buyer], you can try something like this;

Feel free to use these templates as well...

-Hi [name of prospect], we noticed you have a need [identify need] and we would really be glad to help out. Would you be willing to connect with us?

-Hi [name of prospect], we hope this comes at the right time. We have noticed your activeness on this app and we would like to have you on our friend list, would you like to connect with me/us?

Note that all template statements are introductory and not sales phrases; you do not just want to dive into introducing offers just immediately, instead warm them up and try to familiarize your brand with them, engage when you feel they are most active. This approach takes time and won't lead to sales over night but if done with enough patience, you can easily turn a stranger to your friend.

"Learn to build relationship, it makes selling easier"

When you build relationship, you will know the best time to introduce your offer and don't forget to ask for their opinion on your product as this will make them spill out their minds, that way you can say for sure what they are thinking and how you can come in.

Always post word quotes, quiz, videos and infographics, amazing and fascinating statistics, behind the scenes of your products, customer stories and case studies. All these makes the prospect get warm and emotionally attached to you brand.

Another way to get along with your new prospect is the introduction of free training on a specific topic, to reduce cost of hosting people, you can do this virtually by organizing a program or by creating a tutorial video on how to use your product, another option is to host a live webinar by sharing your webinar link on your feeds on social media and group chats and forums.

"I know a lot of you must be thinking of giveaway right now... well Giveaway is one of the ways but for people that possess financial power (Owo, Ego, Kudi)"

During this training and webinar, give room for questioning which will be answered at the end of the session, this way you have been able to engage them and that will open ways for more sales opportunities. Reasons why selling on social media is more advisable to practice,

Just to mention few...

- ❖ Faster conversion rates

- ❖ Reduces contact time i.e. you can contact prospects immediately

- ❖ Increases number of leads

- ❖ Strengthens relationships between the seller and the buyer

- ❖ Shorter sales cycle i.e. sales can be made almost immediately and the relationship still stands.

Honestly, the List is Endless. But let's keep digging...

Sales is a game of numbers, the higher the number of prospects turned clients, the higher the amount of revenue you get, your activeness on social media really has a lot to do in this journey.

"And your best bet right now is social media"

The use of social media for sales is underrated as many people do not even know where to start, all we probably know is how to send messages and respond, which is a good thing but we have to start using that to make sales.

When a prospect is willing to buy anything, they turn to social media either to seek a solution or to get a wider view of advice. Please note public opinion matters a lot. For this journey to be successful, you need to develop a plan of action or what we all know as a strategy.

This starts by finding prospects that are similar to your existing customer, introducing yourself as an expert in what you do by sharing knowledge and facts on your page, everyone loves to interact with someone that shows a sense of responsibility and knows what they are doing. Building long term relationships via social media is what social media selling should be about.

Anyways the story continues; let's get a little deeper....

How do we map our customer to build long term relationship?

MAPPING CUSTOMERS

This is the documentation of process where a total stranger becomes your brand's biggest prospect or customer. From stranger to buyer to loyal customer and then hopefully they begin to refer your product to other people. Yes, sales and marketing has changed but one thing hasn't changed "HUMANS AND THEIR BELIEF".

We have to understand how humans relate and how they think, study their psychology and emotion, it is very important for your brand growth.

"As a man, when you go out to meet a lady on a first date, you probably cannot propose marriage because chances of that being possible are very slim. It takes time to understand each other and this process is called courtship or dating. In marketing, it is called mapping"

When what you are doing is not working, you could be selling the wrong product to the wrong audience or probably your product is out rightly bad (Not delivering Value) or the problem is your messaging (Your manner of converting them). It all boils down to "sequence".

Let's quickly identify and digest process of mapping our customers... I promise it won't be boring...

Stage 1: Creation of great content for public awareness

Before anyone can patronize you, they have to know that your brand exists. Right? How can they know your brand exists?

This is the stage where a prospective customer gets to know you exist and might start to learn or know about your product. After all, no one was born automatically knowing about Unilever or Multichoice. It all happened with the right marketing and publicity

"That is why you see big product like apple spending millions of dollars on it brand awareness. They just want everyone to be aware and they are consistent about it....

Please check the internet to confirm the Apple gist...Lol"

.

Creation of great content comes with the zeal of trying to fix a particular problem or explaining how a product has been used or how it can be used to solve a problem; remember this must be created to steal audience attention and meet the need of their emotion.

When you sell good products with appealing content and packaging, the consumer tends to spread the good news themselves without being told or persuaded.

"Garri ijebu for example…. Lol. Don't laugh, have you

asked yourself who is bankrolling it advertisement? No one, but because people see value in it they speak well of it'

When creating content try to view from the public's point of view, particularly what they will feel or how the product will impact their lives. Most times when I create contents, I ask myself questions if the content I have just designed would convert me. Always ask yourself questions before launching that content. If it's worth it, Launch, if it is not trash it and recreate another one.

.

Stage 2: engagement and conversation

Engagement occurs as a result of your activeness and the passion to make your brand known. To make your prospects know you, you have to be consistent with posting your content online and engaging in conversations.

As a small-scale business owner, this approach alone cannot publicize your product, you have to adopt every approach available to you both outbound and electronically (hand bills, flyers, banners etc.)

"If it requires you sending a Hi first on the internet or approaching outbound, please do it... It doesn't cost you anything"

Your prospective customer is now aware of your brand but at this stage they do not trust you; they do not know you just yet and they obviously have not developed any likeness for you or your brand.

This is the point where you prove yourself and introduce your product i.e. sell your true story right with the available marketing mix elements like the provision of educative, entertaining and informative content.

"Don't seem desperate at this point, take it slow… make sure to read and understand your prospect point here, no room for mistakes"

This is a continual process that must not stop half way, if you must stop then you must have another strategy to implement. Create captivating content such as, how to use your product and what your product does. This way your prospect can relate and interact more with your content.

Stage 3: How to make them believe you and subscribe

At this stage your prospective customer already know you and has given you the audience needed to express yourself. Deploy your best persuasive techniques here and make sure you win the prospect over. If you fail to get the prospect's contact details here, then all your time and resources from stage one to stage three is gone, you will never hear from them again. Never!

Ask for that contact info here. Don't sleep on it.

Still, don't be surprised if some didn't give out their personal details, it is not easy to trust these days, especially in this era of internet fraudsters using difference means to siphon people hard earned money. People just want to be safe with their money and private information.

"But you have to try your best... No new prospect out

there, one way or the other someone is trying to convert that person you're talking to so don't lose your chance"

After engaging prospects, get them to subscribe. You do this by getting their contact information like email addresses or phone numbers with their permission to contact them again in the future.

Please note that every engagement does not guarantee sales but every engagement can guarantee leads for future sales. If they cannot buy today, do not lose such an encounter by letting go, try to get their details and profile such prospects.

Most times, it is an in-depth but brief introduction of your content that they feel would solve their problems. Always be ready to offer value so as to get back.

Stage 4: when they make the first stage to convert

After getting the attention of your prospects, some of them might want to increase the level of their commitment.

The conversion stage of the customer value process is about acquiring buyers or ramping up the commitment level of the prospects. This is not about earning profit just yet; it is about business growth and sustainability.

This is the part where every sales person wants to pay attention...

This is an important and most delicate stage in the Customer Value Journey and one that frustrates many business owners the most. *Let me break it down*;I mean this is the stage where most business option out.

The secret to success in this stage is to deploy what we call new entrant or entry point offers. These kinds of offers are specifically designed to give the new prospects absolute value without forcing them to put too much in the game.

Let's take a typical example, YouTube as a brand pops notifications every now and then; persuading audience into accepting their product free trail for one month. This strategy tells you to subscribe free for the next one month then you can now decide to continue after free service.

What they want to do is to gently and carefully bring you into the system and later turn to be a paying customer. If you refuse their offer, they will leave you to enjoy their basic package by watching videos then at another time probably another day, same notification pops again, they are careful with the way they do this so as not to piss you off.

This converting stage is not a time to ask your client to invest a substantial amount of money in a product. At this stage they will still be careful with the way they deal with you and you might be losing money during this stage on the prospects you acquire as buyers.

This is one of the costliest marketing processes a company would ever embark on.

For this same reason, some companies are ready to hijack a customer from you if you are not willing to commit the customer.

This is the truth... Let me gist you about the church I attended sometimes back!

I remembered visiting a particular church for the first time, I wouldn't want to mention name, and they called us out being a first timer and get us seated at the front roll where the elders' seats, the church gave us some church packages including food. Honestly, I felt really on top of the world, I felt special.

Even after I stopped going to the church for reason best known to me, I still keep telling my true experience about the church. You know what the church has successfully done?

They had converted me.

Show care and emotional concern towards your prospect and be consistent about it, sales will pursue you hands down.

Stage 5: actual value when they buy your product and excited

The excitement stage is when you make sure the customer gets value for their money. If your product does not bring about satisfaction post consumption, such customers might not be willing to continue patronizing you.

"Customer experience is key as this is what brings about customer retention"

The question you might probably have on your mind now is, how do you ensure your customer has a good experience?' This depends on your product and brand consumer satisfaction plan; make sure you have quality products at all point in time and good service delivery.

If you have a bad product but an outstanding marketing program, the same speed at which the business grows is the same speed at which the business fails. The goal is to document a customer; a customer value journey per seller, document and follow up ONE CUSTOMER AT A TIME.

One loyal customer is worth more than 10 visitors, so treat that one customer like a King. The excitement that one customer gets is what makes the customer keep coming back. At all points in time, ensure to make customer experience your priority.

Stage 6: Retention and Referral

At this point you have one loyal customer that is willing to buy your product over any competitive product in the market.

At this stage you have invested money, time, and resources into acquiring such customers and kept with the consistent habit of making sure they get value.

Now you are sure of loyalty and trust; this is when you can introduce other relevant products where you can maximize your profit.

"Feel free with your loyal customer, don't stop rendering value; they will always choose you over competitive brand"

THE CONCEPT OF SALES, MONEY AND ENTREPRENEUR

I am sure you must have read a lot of books or attended seminars on how to make sales or how you can build your business revenue, but no one seems to be disclosing exactly how this is been done or they discussed but not ready to take you by the hand to help you do it yourself.

Well, do not blame them as only few knows the philosophy surrounding these concepts.

Sales concept is a very technical one as you will have different opinions and approaches on what works for A and not works for B. it is now left to you to decide if it will work for you or not.

I have always preached something, before starting a business it is important to do a thorough market survey, this is to know what the market wants and the best way in which you can deliver such product to the target market. (I do not mean go to oyingbo market and start doing survey, life is easy now, you can do it online).

"Business owners can leverage on the free Google form to construct a survey questions and share with friends and family on social media. Keep sharing same form link for minimum of 7 days, by then you would have documented enough response to do the analysis about your target market. How do I create a survey link? It's simple…. Just log into your Gmail account on your

browser, create another tab and click on Google forms. Click on it and there you have a plain sheet to design a market survey"

A lot of people start business and realize they are not making sales; the big mistake is starting a business just because you love the business or because you see people doing it and you decide to do it as well not considering the consumers of such business.

Marketing your business for sales can be a very strenuous thing, considering the amount of time, money and energy that will be channelled into the business, I am sure you would not want to start a business and liquidate almost immediately especially after ruining your money on advertisement of what people do not need.

Businesses especially those that do not have the financial strength to keep consistency in running paid ads must do a market survey. Just pay attention to your environment through survey and see what people needs most.

The essence of this is to solve the issue of having a business and not having a buyer.

"One of the secrets to sales is to identify a multitude of hungry audience, then create a product for that audience, sales will chase you hands down. Not create product for a market that do not exist."

I know it is hard to think of what to do that people wants and it is not yet in saturation, it is very hard but I can guarantee that the moment you come about such idea, the chances of it been successful is high.

"The truth of the matter is, all of us cannot be successful entrepreneurs, and some will fail almost immediately as they've started while some will one day shares their success stories. Our choices of business are different but we must be a rational thinker when it comes to selecting our choices of business"

Ok, let me tell you a simple idea of a good business sense as suggested by a millionaire friend but I didn't venture into it because I was not financially buoyant and of course time constraint as at that time but I must say it is a nice idea.

Opening a construction firm in a rural area very close to Texas where you know there is a site development i.e constructions are ongoing in that vicinity, as flaccid as this idea may seems, I can say it is not yet saturated and I have this strong feeling that it will scale.

Lately, a lot of investors have been preaching about owning a house and becoming a landlord, if you must build a house then you'll need building materials, it will be much easier if you have them very close. Sales get easier when competition is low.

"The idea is to solve a problem and your solution will sell."

What if you already have a business?

Well, I have not said you have made the wrong choice of business or you can't make sales, but truth be told, you have to do things differently to make more sales.

How do you do things differently?

You have to follow the process as explained above (Customer Mapping) and also the approaches that will be discussed as you read on and be disciplined to follow the process strictly.

Let's interact more...

Another hint on how to help boost your understanding when it comes to understanding how sales and money works for your existing business.

"To generate more money, pay someone to keep your business running while you focus on developing and growing the business."

The logic about the business game is simple; the employees want to retain their job so that they can continue to provide food for their families, so they have to work while they get paid for the work done. They see to the daily running of the business, and as a result, your business becomes their priority.

What do you believe in?

Our educational system was designed to make us believe so much in the 9-5 job to the extent that we just want to go to school, graduate with good grades and find a job. Leaving us with the rat race mentality; that is if you're even lucky enough to secure a job on time.

I called this the catch 22 approach; where we are being trapped from doing what we love the most or being with those we love the most.

Most times when we get home after our daily endeavours we feel really tired and just want to go to bed and get prepared for following day. The truth we all are aware of but wouldn't admit is that 9-5 jobs are not sustainable in the long run.

Well, we can't blame ourselves; this is the situation we find ourselves. What am I saying in essence? *Listen to me carefully*

"If you keep trading your time for money, you can never be rich"

I am not advising you quit your 9-5 job, in fact you need the resources from that job to kick-start your ideas and dreams; but it is that time start thinking on how to tap into the wealth of expansion and digitalisation.

Successful people would prefer to invest their money into human resources in terms of expansion and wait for the long run to start making profit. From the list of the wealthiest people on earth, none of them is handling all the role in their organization, other than the most important task of foreseeing and making strategic decisions in their businesses, they spend extra hours working even after the regular closing hour just to see that the business keep going.

"I know you might be speculative by saying these people own a conglomerate of business and you don't expect them to do everything themselves, but the shocking news is that these people believe in process flow and the law of large numbers from people working with them to their customer base. If they had not started investing in people to get their job done, they would not be where they are today. You can start from just one staff to ten then grow later"

These set of people have been able to tweak the hand of time. Let me explain what I mean here.

As human, we all are entitled to 24 hours in a day which makes us exposed to almost equal productivity level. We are also entitled to work for minimum of 8 hours in a day depending on our kind of job. These set of people knew if they need more money than anyone else, they have to buy time for themselves; how can they achieve this? The only way is to own a business where they have more hands working for them, hence more money.

I have seen a business start up owner that pays salary of employees for six months before the business finally scale; only few people can take such risk

Let's take an illustrative example of how some individuals are more likely to survive and make massive sales more than every other human;

on a regular basis an entrepreneur and the employee have 8hours each in a day to work (9am-5pm job), assuming you have 10 people in different location or even in same location working for you, that means you have 10 employees multiply by 8 hours to give you 80 hours exceeding the 8hours you have to yourself.

Every successful people in this world have leverage on this pattern to makes sales and get results in their respective business. These people also did something almost in the same pattern.

"Selecting business of wants and deploying the expansion techniques."

Their kinds of business are things we can do without, i.e. we can do without their product for another alternative. They deals with mostly business of wants; thing we do not use our head to do but our emotion.

Few examples are Amazon, Coca-Cola, Twitter and Facebook amongst others, all these are brands/products we can do without, we can survive without them but yet we still choose to go for them because we made that decision of picking these variables with our emotion, not our head. They are now a necessity in our lives

"When you have things that people want, you automatically make sales, sales will patronise you without advertisement."

On the other hand,

Poorly oriented people have the belief that when they employ a professional person to manage their business, it is waste of funds or they are getting cheated.

This is why they always want to handle all aspects of their business personally; from production to advertisement to delivery. At the end of the day, they mess it all up or get tired along the line.

The fact is, with proper management techniques, you get to see other people doing your job better than you would do it, without having the feelings of losing money or being cheated.

Don't get this wrong,

What I am insinuating from the whole explanation above is that, you cannot get everything done alone; you cannot be everywhere at the same time, you need at least one more person assisting you in executing your plans. No matter how small your business is, get someone to help out.

"Start doing things with an extra hand, two heads are better than one."

You can place the employee on a commission-based flow or pay wages or salary but stop the habit of getting everything done yourself; this can be really exhaustive.

I don't expect you to believe everything you have read in this handbook, as I am aware you are entitled to your opinions and believe, but I will advice you add this knowledge to the vast knowledge you had acquired earlier or elsewhere and work on testing these knowledge.

Let me tell you a short story

This story is about a woman I have lived with for 15 solid years.

Lol quite a long time huh?

Yes, you can say that again. I have lived with her because she is my foster mom. I will fast forward to why I have decided to tell this story.

She is a very hard-working woman that works Monday to Sunday. I know you must be wondering if she does not rest. Yes, she rests; but on a Monday just for half a day. She is in a business of WANT; she sells fresh catfish at the market (Igando market to be precise).

Sales of catfish business is not what you'd see everywhere in the market unlike cold rooms for frozen foods. People love to eat catfish pepper no doubt, but this is a want and not a need. They can do without catfish pepper soup, right? But their decisions of purchasing the catfish are triggered by their emotions.

So, let me continue my story ….

A lot of people became so sceptical about how she accumulates her wealth; some even said maybe she had joined some kind of stuff unknown to the regular and professional ethics *(I hope you know what I am saying here…. Voodoo!).*

All I could say for sure is that she gets new staffs to work for her almost every two months. But what does that mean? Nothing! Especially to a clueless person like me as at that time, I became worried and decided to ask her one afternoon how she made her wealth and about the things a lot has been saying.

She responded saying "I know"

She said she knows because she is aware a lot of people will find it hard to believe how everything works for her and this is her little trade secret which I will be sharing with you now..

She said and I quote **"I employ people to do what only me will do, but manage them all the way I will manage myself"** this simply means she believes in law of large number and expansion; she trained her employees to be as good as her.

What she has done is to expand and monitor her business. Her only job is to supervise then think on what she can do to make the business grow. Believe me, the only job that she does is the biggest task ever as an entrepreneur

Her pattern is simple, every human has 24 hours in a day, but successful people who know the value of investing in people to have more than 24 hours to them. What this simply means is that the higher the numbers of people working for you, the higher you will be able to tweak the hands of time to get results.

I hope you are not getting this wrong

Note that different approaches work for different kind of business, what I cited earlier was just an example of an approach that works for an entrepreneur.

 If you do not have a business right now and you are thinking of what to do or you are scared of taking risk of starting a business, pending the time you make up your mind to finally start, I have a simple advice for you, start investing more on yourself, your health and people; all these can be monetise in the long run and do not fall short of sales.

"Naturally, you will always sell"

Expansion of business can mean more sales and revenue but, but this can only be done when you know you have a good knowledge of your market and you have a good stand of your present business.

Don't think of expansion when you can barely scale the one you have at hand, you can expand when you have a business of want but the truth is Expansion is not for everybody; yes... it is not for everybody.

Always practicalise anything you've learnt before launching your approach.

WANT, NEED AND SALES

Economics will define needs as something we cannot do without while want to be what we can do without. *Right?*
Yes, you're right!

But when it comes to selecting a kind of business to give you sales, select a business of want to a business of need. Need is limited as want is unlimited.

To make sales, Want is now, need is later. One of the major reasons why a lot of us is not making sales is because we are doing the wrong business.

 Sometimes around early 2019, I needed money so badly to settle some Bills, keep my life running, even as an employee to a reputable firm I feel the urge to have a passive stream of income, take note of the word PASSIVE" so I thought of doing a business but I was wrong about the business I chose.

Yes, you're right!

But when it comes to selecting a kind of business to give you sales, select a business of want to a business of need. Need is limited as want is unlimited.

To make sales, Want is now, need is later. One of the major reasons why a lot of us is not making sales is because we are doing the wrong business.

Sometimes around early 2019, I needed money so badly to settle some Bills, keep my life running, even as an employee to a reputable firm I feel the urge to have a passive stream of income, take note of the word PASSIVE" so I thought of doing a business but I was wrong about the business I chose.

Don't forget I said I needed money so badly, so any business I must choose must be a business that'll have massive response as per what people want.

Guess the business that I chose?

I ventured into pig (piggery) farming.*I must say with all sincerity that I regret my decision.*

Don't get me wrong on this, I never said pig farming is not a lucrative business, as a matter of fact, this is one of the best investment decisions anyone can make. *I have been there....* But my choice of decision as a young guy looking for passive means of income was wrong.

I invested around one million naira into a business that'll be ready in span of 5 to 6 months. I didn't realize that it was a wrong move as at then, so I waited patiently while switching between my corporate job and checking on my animals. It wasn't an easy task for me as I'll have to check in on weekends to see if the staffs are doing the business properly.

At this point, I had no choice but to wait, I knew I had made the wrong decision and there is no going back.

On the 4th month of massively fattening my stock for pay day, I got a call from work and it was the saddest news I received that year,

"Oga 2 pigs don die o" terrible news keep flooding in...

I felt so sad and furious because I felt the pigs are matured and are not prone to any sickness. I left work that fateful day to see what had happened. We took the carcass of the pig for lab testing. The unthinkable had happened; my flock was infested with Swine fever.

At that point, my regret over choosing a wrong business tripled. I had to meet people to buy them off; I can't even start talking about the prices these people started negotiating a one-million-naira business.

I accepted my losses and moved on, but I know not everyone will find it easy to move on, some might even kick the bucket in the process. The essence of this is just to put our attention into the choice of business to go for.

"A want cannot be an investment; an investment is a Need."

We need to invest for later not now. Any business decision you're making, always think of what people want first before need. A want will always drive more sales than need decision for busying things of want is always from the heart not from the head.

We buy want because our emotion dictates for us not our head. Lol

"I remembered on day coming from the office really famished, I perceived an aroma which I traced and it led me down to an asun joint, I bought quite a large amount and ate while on the bus heading home. What I needed at that moment that could satisfy my hunger is food, but my emotion led me into buying an appetizer. Lol I finished eating and started regretting why I wasted such money on that thing which I knew if I had used that same money to buy food, I will be satisfied and still have some change left with me"

When you have a business of want and you know it's doing well, then the next thing to do is to think of expansion. I know someone reading this has a contrary opinion, anyways it's your opinion and you're entitled to it, but try to absorb the positive knowledge from this experience.

I hope you're not getting my message wrong still...

Some business of want is saturated as well; a typical example is the food business. Viewing centre business, car dealer business, some requires huge capital while some requires little capital.

PRODUCT PERSUASION AND PERSUASIVE TECHNIQUES IN SALES

Persuasion is the art of convincing a prospect to see reason to go for your brand. We all are aware of the numerous, different and similar brands out there; it all depends now on your negotiation and persuasive skills to convert a prospect to your client. Now you have a prospect that is willing to know your terms and offers, but how persuasive are you or how likely you are able to convert such a prospect to a paying client.

We are exposed to a whole lot of product persuasion every day of our lives in different forms and approaches. Every day we get exposed to advertisements of products and offers online. Some even go as far as giving price slashes and free samples, just to get the attention of prospects and lure them into purchasing your products and converting them to permanent customers.

"Most of the time when prospects ask questions about your brand, such prospects are trying to negotiate or compare your brand with other similar products or brands they have come across before, don't over fix your price here as this might be a total turn off for the prospect. Mastering the art of persuasion is not an easy task but it is what every sales representative should understand. For increase in sales, your negotiation skills must be top notch and well structured"

Persuasion is not something that is useful for just sales personnel alone; it is something that is needed in our everyday activities.

How often do your prospects call up on you and say they would like to know how good your product is? Not often I guess, and this is more reason why your persuasion skills must be at its best. Food vendors want us to buy their sumptuous meals while hairdressers want us to buy their hair products or get their latest hair deals.

However, learning the subtle art of persuasion can help in achieving goals in life. You might aspire to be a great negotiator outside marketing or you might want to convince your child to eat a particular food which he or she does not like or even convince your employer to give you that salary raise at work.

"Persuasion is a psychological thing that needs to be carefully observed and rolled out. Every advert we see on our TVs, billboards, newspaper, etc. has some form of persuasion techniques embedded in them to convert a prospect; some of these techniques include the percentage cuts, price slashes, free enrolments, free trials, product trials and many more"

Let us look quickly look into the different persuasion techniques and how they can be used to convert prospects to paying clients.

Posture and appearance

Do you know that the way you stand or present yourself both offline and online respectively can help turn a prospect to a client or turn a prospect off totally? We can call this power pose. (Physical appearance is only applicable offline i.e. it only works when you are on field or a sales representative rather than being an online marketer).

You can also reflect your power pose when making a video content for online visibility; perish your fear, it is just a video session, nothing serious (I'd always have a brief conversation and laugh before getting started) , do not show sign of weakness, be bold and bright. Also, while having a good profile and presenting yourself as a professional is applicable online.

I have an engineer friend that would borrow a car to meet clients and seal deals... Sick right?

Let me tell you how rich people think, not even wealthy people alone (people generally) I don't want you to be sentimental about this; you can quote me contrary if this doesn't happen 75% of times.

-People would prefer to give job or patronize a good-looking person than someone looking hungry and unkempt.

-People would prefer to seal contract with someone that comes to submit business proposal with a car to someone that came on bike.

I always advice sales representative to wear an attractive eau de cologne perfume, nice not too expensive wrist watch depending on your pocket but definitely not a fake wrist watch. Smell nice, let people have a feel of your amazing presence out there. Even with a bad day for the prospect, they will still give you listening ears (This only works offline)

This is not living fake lifestyle as we fondly say; this is about presenting yourself in a way that is compelling. Don't blame people that makes this kind of selection by look or appearance, psychology is at its peak. They believe hungry looking people will not execute their job well or even disappear with their money, unlike good looking person that present professionalism and good look. When you have a professional profile on social media, prospect will trust you more.

This is not the time to debate, like I said earlier this happens most of the time….

When you approach a prospect, the first thing the prospect looks at is your confidence, approach and how well you can defend your product. No one is going to be convinced or listen attentively to a weak and an unkempt individual. Showing a great sense of authority can convince a prospect that you are a goal getter. Dress neatly and smartly, stand upright with your head up and introduce yourself properly.

Standing at akimbo is a total turn off for customer; they can easily predict how weak you are and this would adversely affect your business. A good stance shows a great level of confidence and depicts the aura to trust your product. Posing a form of confidence and command reflect in the way that you speak as well. Speak politely and confidently with a little bit of smile to hide your nervousness.

"I know one of the biggest problems is the inability to speak to people and not freak out especially when introducing a product to a stranger, while the prospect listen, you'd imagine if what you were saying is right or its total crap to your audience, well the truth is, even the best speakers in the whole world get scared at first, but with proper training, you can learn to be confident despite the fear and nervousness"

What I do is simple , before getting to a prospect both online and offline, I rehears what I want to say, at times I speak to myself testing how it will sound; if it doesn't sound lame or stupid to me, then I can test it.

SOCIAL PROOFS

Social proof is no doubt is one of the best and still working persuasion techniques. Having your clients write a review as well as testimonials on your page or website is very important to any business brand that has the vision to remain in business.

The psychology behind human reasoning is very powerful and technical; many of us will likely buy a product because a friend of ours already bought it and used it and you can ask how the product works or you have probably seen how the product works. Our decisions at times are based on the experience of others. To continue making steady sales always reference high profile clients that you have worked or used your brand in comparison to your competitor brand, this way you will change the mind of prospects and persuade them to buy from you. NOTE: do not attempt a fake social proof.

AGITATION AND SOLVE.

Agitation and solve is an old technique that still works very well. This is the act of identifying the prospect problem, then talking in emotional terms to help solve the problem. When you highlight a prospect's problem, it makes them feel anxious about the problem they are facing and how it has been left unsolved. Then, make all the feeling of anxiousness, fear and hopelessness go away by replacing them with feelings of happiness and hope.

When you approach a prospect to convert them, always make them understand that you know what they are going through and you can imagine yourself in their situation. This way, fifty percent of the element of doubt is gone, they will immediately tend to trust you and open up to you.

"I remembered my days on the field as a revenue collector representative for a power firm, my persuasive skills were simple, I just assumed I were in their position, made them understand that i knew exactly how they feel

because I was once in their position, explained how I could solve their problems and voila! We became friends, exchanged numbers, and just like that, conversion of a prospect into a client takes place. This technique seems a bit simple but it is a power tool which I feel you can master'

4. "It's their choice" approach

Most people do not like to be told what to do, what not to do and how things should be done. We all want to be in charge and make decisions on our own. This is something that is very common with humans and how they behave. At this point, when striking for conversion and sales you have to stop using an aggressive approach and always remind the prospect that it is their choice to make a decision.

"A prospect can tell you what they feel is right and what they want. Never turn them down, try to work in accordance to their terms. Always reassure them that it is their choice, this way they feel in charge and want to stay in charge. When a prospect feels calm and is the boss in

the conversation then you can introduce mouth-watering offers to them, if they are in charge, they will buy your idea without stress"

5. Limiting your choices of offers to prospects

When you are trying to convert a prospect, always try to limit your choices as too many options overwhelm your prospects and you might end up not closing any deal.

Content marketing deals with persuasiveness and accuracy. Pick a few choices and market them well. People are more likely to make final decisions with concise options. Honestly from my experience, you are not required to talk too much as against the usual notation that marketers must talk more to convert a client.

"What I do is limit my options to the ones I know the prospect is likely to go for, ask questions about the choices of the prospect, then introduce my options as a solution to the identified problems. Learn to ask questions so as to know how to offer solutions'

6. Giving more than You Offer

This is an approach whereby you make it seem as if you are giving more than you are offering. To convince buyers, you must offer mouth-watering deals that will attract the buyers' attention. Learn to dramatize your ideas and pitching to make it more realistic and persuasive.

Make the prospect visualize how the product or service will result in better outcome for them, how your ideology has been able to solve their problem. Some brand adopts the use of buy 2 get one free or buy two for the price of one.

"A typical beer product that needs audience would give this kind of offer by saying, buy two get one free, but most times this offer is psychological in nature as the price of two beers actually covers for three beers. I will say everything needs and works with psychology"

PROVIDING EXCELLENT CUSTOMER SERVICE EXPERIENCE

Customer service experience is one thing we all have to put into consideration during the customer value process and this is not the job of the customer service team alone but the duty of the entire brand. One negative experience could ruin a flawless relationship between a brand and her prospect since first and last impression matters a lot in service delivery.

What does this mean?

This simply means, when you meet a prospect, you should apply professionalism while dealing with them during the entry stage and still maintain said professionalism after they become a customer. If you have a customer and they are not being managed well, the tendency of losing such a customer is very high.

Excellent customer service delivery is a consistent process that must involve meeting and exceeding customer's expectations at all times. If the quality of service has been set, lowering it will be a disappointment on the part of the customer. Hence maintaining a standard of operation (SOP) is one key factor that needs to be considered.

For customer retention, it should always be a priority for every member of the team to exceed customer expectations; when you beat their expectations positively, they become loyal and help your brand grow. Target creating a WOW! Experience.

Feel great right? Let's continue.

Have you thought of swift ways to create magical moments for customers? Magical moments for customers are those special moments in which a customer can always brag about out when it comes to using your product. Most times, it makes the customer feel unique and cared for. Imagine a customer comes in with a complaint that seems to be overwhelming and you have them sit, relax, have a cup of water or soft drink while you solve the issue?

CREATING A CUSTOMER SERVICE CULTURE

If I was asked what customer service is, I will simply say it is a way in which brand efforts are being centred on the customer (the brand is about the customer). Every brand that dreams to grow big must have the capacity to manage and make its customer feel unique in every way; this can be achieved by having the right and professional set of employees that have all the qualities of a care agent and have the ability to lead a team and also create valuable culture.

Every member must make it obligatory to drive the brand to success....

Creating a perfect customer service culture is very crucial as it is the sole heart of the business, all the basics of the business must be understood very well and this will have a great effect on the conversion rate.

Your vision as a brand must be spelt out and well understood by every member of the team. At this point the team should be given the freedom to do the right thing and make it work according to the vision and mission of the brand.

Customer service culture is all about the brand and how they can serve the client better. Hiring should be based on merit i.e. who will best represent the interest of the company. Whether you are a new entrant into the business or an existing operator, customer focused culture has to be everyone's business from the gatekeeper to the CEO. Training also assists the team to grow and know how best to treat their customers.

Do you know there is a way the human mentality is being designed?

Human beings have a way of thinking, "The way you treat me is the way I will treat you". When you treat your customer like a king, they will keep coming back for more. Document feedback from employees and work on them. With all we have talked about so far it would be unjust if we didn't mention motivation and celebration of success as this is what keeps the employee going in terms of excellent service delivery.

USING ALL AVAILABLE COMMUNICATION CHANNELS

To provide an unbeatable customer experience, you need to get information, offers and products to your customers in the most available and easiest ways. This involves the usage of social media platforms, emails, documentation of promotional contents, community forums etc.

This present age have brought about a lot of advancements in technology, innovation and a simple way of reaching people so fast; this is about being at the right place at the right time using the right approach to reach a wider audience. The old way of relying on calls alone is fast going into extinction when all of your customers spend almost 50% of their time on social Medias and other digital platforms.

"As a brand, using social media and other digital platforms, conversion should be top priority. This is an era of self-services where you can create an FAQ question online and also respond with the answer. This way customer would not have to stay on the long queue to be attended to; they can search for their question online and get the response to the questions automatically"

Explainer videos of product and services can be documented and placed online for your audience's attention. For example: A customer finding it hard to load a recharge card would not have to go through the stress of contacting the customer care team on phone and wait while the phone connects, or maybe wait at the long queue of the customer service center just to load a recharge card. Such customer can always type that same question online and all information on FAQs (Frequently Asked Questions) pop up and you can self-service.

Every interaction has to be managed one at a time. You can decide to follow a simple approach by delivering what the customer expects, and then you ask extra questions to make sure you understand exactly what the customer needs for clarity sake and also be proactive enough to answer the questions the customer is yet to ask. Always end strong,

Your first impressions and last impressions are really lasting impressions. Please take note.

"The other day I was at a mall with few people on the queue waiting to be checked into a cinema hall. It got to a

point that I almost collapsed looking at the long line ahead of me. The cinema could have options to use a barcode where customers can easily buy tickets online and get scanned before entering the cinema hall. Such a move would have been more efficient, cost effective, easy to use, reached a wider audience and also be a self-service option"

MEASURING PRODUCT SUCCESS AND TRACKING PERFORMANCE INDEX

One thing small scale or growing SMEs do not consider priority is the need to measure their success and track their performance. Many people just sell without taking their time to look at where they got bad reviews about their service and what they should fix up.

"You might think your business is doing well but in the real sense you can do much better than you used to.

In tracking specific metrics, you need details, data of how you can serve your audience better. This can be achieved by the use of a survey or questionnaire, asking specific questions online to get response"

This way, you can identify what is working for you so you replicate or put more effort in that line to increase your revenue margin. You can also find out what is not working for you, either drop it or pinpoint areas where you need to improve.

You can start by asking simple questions to be shared as mail to the employees; questions like did the customer problem get solved?

How many times did the customer have to call in before the complaint was resolved?

If your customers have a question to ask, they only ask once and after that, if they don't get a positive or relieving response, they might decide to leave your brand for a relative brand. You don't want that to happen, would you? Then, take the baton and do it right by measuring your performance as well as your failure.

They both are important for your business sustainability. When you're excelling, do more and focus on your strength, if you are doing bad, focus on where you need to improve or when you need to call it a quit.

CONTENT MARKETING

According to research, it is ascertained that Content marketing produces three times more leads than paid search. It has both smaller up-front costs and bigger long-term benefits. Creating good content for your product is the best that could ever happen to your organization, this is always a long-term motive.

Furthermore, as time goes on, content continues to perform with no extra expenses required. In my words, I term it the "domino effect". Meanwhile, paid search needs a continual cash flow to maintain results; a continual cash flow that does not have an ending. Content marketing drives six times higher conversions than traditional marketing for converting people into leads and leads into customers. Content is king. You can blend content marketing with social media; the average of your prospective customers is on social media.

"To break down what Content marketing means to a layman, I would say it is a blend of educational and promotional techniques to drive a converting gaol"

Content marketing gives detailed information of a product in a well-structured and simple manner. It's a kind of marketing mix element that aims to orientate the audience of your product, what the product tends to solve rather than raising your curiosity on what your product could solve.

Content marketing basically is not about the product or service; it is absolutely about your audience. Content marketing includes things like educational fliers and banners, e-books, videos etc designed to educate or convert a prospect.

These are things that answer specific questions people have and provide them with what they cannot get elsewhere. So before creating content for your brand kindly sit down and think of how the customer can understand you in a simple and precise manner, Content marketing takes a lot of work, persistence and patience.

STORY TELLING

I have used an approach of storytelling and it works for me every time. In the previous years it has been proven that telling a story about your product converts prospective customers to real clients faster. The act of storytelling about a product is by preaching value with a mixture of emotion and educative content.

"Targeting a client's emotion is a key aspect of marketing. It takes a good content story teller to tell a good story well. You might have a good content story about your product and still not tell it well. Good content is not about good storytelling, it is about telling a good story well"

I recently watched a product pitching from a young inventor to a med company. He was trying to get investors to be interested in his techniques in solving a problem he found lingering.

storytelling about a product is by preaching value with a mixture of emotion and educative content.

"Targeting a client's emotion is a key aspect of marketing. It takes a good content story teller to tell a good story well. You might have a good content story about your product and still not tell it well. Good content is not about good storytelling, it is about telling a good story well"

I recently watched a product pitching from a young inventor to a med company. He was trying to get investors to be interested in his techniques in solving a problem he found lingering.

He pitched his idea to the investors using statistics, facts and data but none of the investors were willing or getting interested in his approach. Until he started talking about the story of why he established his approach, his aim of him establishing that approach and what his approach had solved in the past and what his approach would solve in the nearest future,

"His story was about his friend that died from leukaemia and this was why he used his knowledge as a young scientist to start researching in a drug that can cure leukaemia. He affirms how this innovation can change the entire healthcare system"

The short lesson here is that 'People do not buy what you do or produce; they buy why you do it or why you produced it'

A long story huh?! Sorry about that.

This is why you as a product and content manager should tell more stories about your product. It does not matter whether you are presenting your product to a potential audience who are not familiar with your product.

Irrespective of who your product audience is, they will be more likely to remember the story you tell. Take them on a journey of emotion, why they should care and use your products.

"Those who you are presenting your products to do not necessarily have interest in your stats and data because it

will not stick to their memory; stories stick to memory faster. There is a science around storytelling"

Another strategy in story telling in marketing is the act of asking questions from your prospects while telling the story, this will make the conversation more engaging and will give you a lead on how to respond to your prospect. Asking questions is always the best.

When you ask questions, you are 75% sure of getting a response either YES or NO. When you approach someone for sales, learn to make the conversation interactive. I know it is hard to meet someone for the first time and get the person's attention but this way is the best; you tend to know if the prospect is ready to listen to you or have an opinion about what you have to offer.

Every engagement cannot guarantee sales but every engagement should guarantee relation and leads. Make this your target.

Here's a brief example of Content and using story telling

Let us write content about a popular deodorant so you can have a hint of what good storytelling is and you get to choose which one you would probably go for.

A) Do you have persistent perspiration? Have ordinary deodorants failed you?

Good news! Ever since I started using XYZ deodorant my perspiration has stopped; there is no body odour and my wife gets to love me more.

B) Get XYZ deodorant. It helps stop perspiration and body odour.

I know by now you are more attached to A because it talks more of a story and relates the content to real life happenings. People tend to believe things fast when it feels like it has happened to someone previously or it has been used before. That is why we have product reviews; it gives assurance and trust. It solved a frequently asked question (FAQ) and you have the answer right there with you.

HOW TO GET CLIENTS EVERYWHERE (THE ART OF CONVERTING)

I think we have to say the truth here. People buy from who they like, know and trust. And there is no bigger *secret to sales than greater care.*

To accomplish converting a prospect in a short while, we have to show greater care first, before considering other techniques to converting.

To convert a prospect your content must be highly relatable and educational, this is also applicable to one on one sale.

"Please open your mouth and mind to conversation as this is the only way to driving conversion"

When you engage your prospect, which is when you will be able to identify their needs and then create a solution, asking the right questions to uncover a buyer's affliction and aspiration. Find a balance between talking and listening to steer the conversation in the right direction, convince buyers to see a reason to go with your offer and find a lasting solution to close the lingering gap.

Do not force your product in the heart of your prospect as this will create tense atmosphere. Give your prospect the chance to take a breath and start talking about their aspiration and affliction; this must come after targeting your questions to seeking the prospect's opinion. This session will highlight the various steps to follow to start making sales

1)Qualify your prospect

To qualify your prospect, you have to answer some question which will serve as an indicator to help you plan and lead to amazing conversion response.

I)identify your prospects
ii)Are they a good fit for the product or service that you offer?
iii) Do they really want the kind of product or service that you offer?

iv) Do you think the product or service you are offering will make a significant impact on their lives?

v)Are you ready to learn about your audience with their presence online?

2)Focus on your prospect alone

Your prospects are present everywhere i.e. both online and offline, waiting for your support to solve their problem. Your attention should be given to them at all points in time. The big question is how do you know if they need your attention? How can you predict or guess this when you are not a fortune-teller? Well, with the right question you will get to know what they want and you can devise a solution from your various ranges of products and service offers. If your prospect can't find you, find them.

3) Asking a sensitive qualifying question with their permission

Being a brand that is willing to do well in the industry, you have to create your personalized customized qualifying question to convert. When you do not ask questions, how do you intend to know what these humans are thinking or what their problems are? Please note that you have to ask questions based on your product line. Ask questions related to the list below,

About your product

i)   Have you heard about our product or service? If the prospect hasn't heard about your product, here is your chance to introduce briefly stating the problems your product can solve. You only have limited moment to register your purpose in the prospect's head and I am sure you don't want to mess that up. Be brief and precise.

ii)   What is your experience consuming our product or service?

If the prospect has heard or used your product, that's good news for you. Now is the time to assess the customer's experience consuming your product; at this point, this prospect might possibly have a negative impression about your product, so it is your duty to correct that and make the customer have a good feeling and impression about your product.

iii) Would you like to give our product a try if it solves your problem?

This is applicable when the prospect hasn't heard about any product that could solve their problem. Your product is the messiah and you must give it your best.

"Your prospect might decide to cut you short by having to bring in conversation about a similar product they have used, just let them. Never try to cut them off, instead hear their opinions then ask questions about the similar product. A prospect might be a loyal customer to that

similar product but, with the right questions asked you can win such a prospect over"

Question asking and knowing when to ask questions are very important techniques you should master in marketing to drive sales. These approaches assist you to know the weakness (es) of similar competitive brands. Then you leverage on their weaknesses, preaching your product to be the solution to close that gap.

About similar brand (competitor's product)

    i.   Are you currently a consumer of a similar product or service?

    ii.   If you don't mind sir, will you tell me about the product?

    iii.   What is your experience consuming such a product or service?

    iv.   Are you getting the desired result consuming such product or service?

    v.   Does this similar product or service solve your problem?

Always give ears to your prospects complaints and praises about similar product; the best way to sell is to use your prospects word to structure your pitching deliverables.

4)   Create a solution to the problem

When you have successfully asked questions, now is the time to proffer solution, try to access where they are now and where they are willing to be in terms of product or service satisfaction. The gap between where they are now and where they would like to be is the gap where you have to bridge; this is where your product or service would come to play.

"Their pains and problems are what you want to solve; your emotional and physical contribution is very essential at this point as this is where they will see your brand as their choice. People buy when they are emotionally connected to their future. Don't blow this up"

5)   The great ASK to convert

You can ask a question towards registering your prospect into your program which you are offering as the solution. Offer your solution like this;

"I have a product or service that would help you so much in solving your problem". Would you love to subscribe to our list of happy customers?

Introduce your product here; tell them the value they will receive in consuming your product or service. Everyone is focused on what can solve their problem not the product itself. Also, ensure them that you will walk them through the steps of investing in your product or service and support them each step of the way. The truth is that everyone wants someone to guide them so they don't make a mistake and also not waste money. Then wait patiently for their response.

What if their response is NO?

That is definitely not what anyone wants. Still, you have to understand the reason for their "NO". Ask if they see value in your offer or if they do not see value in your offer to solve the problem. They may have a statement like "I'm scared", "I don't trust the product" or "I don't see a way to pay for this". These are all normal statements and this shouldn't make you give up on converting such a prospect.

Simply thank them for their time and ask if you can check in with them within 30 days to know if they have a change of mind and keep them on the invitation list. This keeps your prospect warm and ready to buy from you. The 30 days grace helps the client to keep calm to trust your brand and also to weigh their option to use your offer.

And if their response is YES?

"Yaaay! Congratulations, you have successfully converted a prospect. Give a warm response and make them

understand that you can't wait to get started with them. All you need now is their enrolment and subscription. After the YES response, every other thing is easy"

6)   It is time to celebrate your Wins!
You have a new prospect and you should acknowledge yourself for your effort. Commit your brand to serving your new client. Make sure to stay in touch via emails, SMS, phone call and be ready to go through this process again to win another prospect to a client.

CONVERSION CALCULATION AND STUDY

One thing to know as a growing brand is to know how to calculate your conversion rate and how to take decisions. The visitors coming to your page or website are regarded as warm lead, and it is now left to your page or website to convert this warm lead to hot leads or paying leads.

"Some leads become hot prospects as soon as they visit your page or website; they like it and immediately bond with your brand and start following you. They immediately get interested in making a purchase when

they ask for delivery options and prices of goods maybe via direct messages or comment section. Some visit your page or website and do not follow your page or buy your product; these guys are referred to as cold prospect or leads"

There are stages to the conversion funnel which include Reach, Engagement, Contacted and Purchase, which can be seen in your insights. The numbers to your reach is always high while the people that engaged is lesser to the reach while those who contacted is way lower than the engaged audience, while those who purchased are always the least. The cold prospects are the ones you need to focus on and try to convince that your product is their best option.

Create content to focus on their curiosity and emotion, ask them questions like how they would love to be serviced or what their opinion is about the product, identify what their constraint is and restructure your approach to deal with this.

There are simple ways to calculate the rate at which you are losing or converting prospect; this can be done using the conversion stages funnels as discussed earlier. Below is a simple illustration

Remember this calculation is based on your page or website insights.

There are four (4) sales funnel stages which includes
- Reach
- Engagement
- Contacted
- Purchase (conversion)

-To calculate for conversion rate, you divide engagement by reach

-to calculate for contacted rate, you divide contacted by new followers

-To calculate for purchase rate, you divide purchase by contacted

INFLUENCER MARKETING

This is also known as relationship building between a brand and influencer to help pitch her product to the public. The brand uses the help of an influencer to persuade highly targeted audience. An influencer helps in promoting a product or service to his audience through the several influencing marketing strategies.

In case you don't know who influencers are and how they operate, let me break it down…

Influencers are people who have taken their time and resources to build their follower base and of course have a cordial relationship with them. Influencers help promote a product at an agreed rate, but still we should have the full knowledge of influencers, and how to select influencers if at all we need one for our brand as the case may be.

Choosing the right influencer for your product is the best decision a brand could ever make. Selecting influencers should be based on how well they make conversions and the numbers of their deliverables to your product. This is what you should look out for when selecting an influencer and not based on the love or likeness you have for such influencer.

Do not pick an influencer based on the number of followers they have as this is not a determinant for conversion. Influencers should be selected based on their product line and what they offer. For example, you have a sliming Tea product and you need audience, the right kind of influencer to promote your product should be a slim or athletic influencer with nice body shape, not an influencer with plump or fat body shape. An influencer with fat or plump body shape cannot converse their audience to buy the product as their audience would not believe the product, as the influencer in question is not using it. The only way they can believe is when you have a slim influencer and can convince the audience saying that is the product he or she uses and they trust their opinions.

Are we on the same page or I should explain further? I heard someone said I should explain further...

Another reason why choosing an influencer based on followers is not a wise idea, there are so many ways in which people get their followers as some of these followers are not real or they are followers based on Bot software designed to generate automated followers; what this simply means is that there is no relationship between the influencer and the audience and some of them might not even be active.

"For you to know what to do in this situation, check the content previously posted by the influencer and how

engaging the post was; check likes and comments, likes and comments are an indication that people are interested in the content that was published"

As a brand aspiring to grow I will advise you focus on Nano influencers and as time goes on and your brand grows you can decide to choose giant influencers in the industry; Nano influencer are internet promoters that have between 1,000 to 10,000 followers as these influencers have higher relationship with their audience and their rates are relatively low.

And do not forget the purpose of this book; to sell your product without sponsored ads but if there is need to use sponsored ads, use a Nano influencer for higher conversion rate. What you tend to gain by using a Nano influencer as a growing brand includes social reach, engagement, brand awareness etc.

To reduce the cost of getting an influencer you can adopt these strategies and this includes the creation of affiliate programs; this is best explained as pay per click i.e. the influencer gets commission based on the number of audience that patronize the brand as a result of influence by the influencer, before this can happen, you have to establish mutually benefitted agreement between you and the influencer.

"You can introduce discount sales by providing discount code. Simply create a promotional code that includes the name of the influencer and the influencer is paid by the numbers of audience converted using the promotional code. An example of an influencer that uses promotional code in Nigeria is @donjazzy for Betway and V Bank"

These influencers share these promotional codes with their audience. Everyone loves a discount and it's a win-win to everybody involved i.e. the brand, the influencer and the Audience. Trust me a promo code is a very fast way to drive sales and also help to measure the numbers of sales made or driven by a particular influencer.

Other methods include designing an influencer name on a product as collaborated efforts at an agreed rate, giving exclusive offers with the help of the influencer etc. You do not want to waste resources and not get results, this kind of influencing is a bit better at converting than automated ads; the reason is simple, influencer method involves someone driving the sales; as prospects get to ask questions and get immediate feedback from the influencer unlike an automated drive that does not involve anyone driving the campaign. Both ways are amazing techniques but do a thorough survey and weigh your options well before taking marketing decisions.

BUILDING YOUR OWN INFLUENCER GROUP

A lot of new businesses out there are scared of losing money ranging from cost of production to advertisement cost, but these costs are normal as they are unavoidable in any start up; but this kind of risk must be calculated well before being taken.

The simple truth about influencing is team work; a lot of influencers out there have a group of people they work with regarded as an influencing team. Have you wondered how an influencer with 100k followers would drop an irrelevant tweet and get automatic engagements while a non influencer with 500k followers would drop a tweet and won't get enough engagements? When you check the analytics of such tweets, you realize a lot of people saw the tweets but did not engage because the tweet is not converting and they do not have the need to engage, but a 100k followers influencer gets almost immediate responses to their tweet, relevant or irrelevant.

The reason is not farfetched, they either have who they work with or have really fantastic content which people find useful. But always have it at the back of your mind that there is secret to every trade. Influencers works with their team to reach more people and also to influence people to join the trend or conversation.

"The human brain is designed to react to people's opinions; people don't love to be the first to start a conversation, but they are quick to give opinion in an ongoing conversation"

Building an influencing team is really not an easy task as I must be honest with you, from the selecting of users with the same zeal and passion as you to the management of these users to make sure everyone is participating in the achievement of the set goal. While you have some working so hard to make sure the goal is attained, you also have those that are not working but want to get paid at the end of everything.

The best way to tackle this kind of irregularity is to set tasks for every member and make sure you track them to see that they work towards it. Some influencers go as far as paying #50 per tweet or post made by a team member.

I will share with you an approach I used on twitter for a campaign which generated over 9 million impressions and over 400 thousand reaches within 5 days. This approach is best used on twitter as it involves the targeting of hashtags on trending pages on twitter.

- Created a group of 15 active twitter users
- Created minimum of 10 engaging content about the campaign with a unique hashtag about the campaign
- Designed 10 engaging fliers about the campaign
- Each member is to drop at least 10 tweets with the flier, written content, and a landing link to your website, page inbox or WhatsApp page; note that this must target the trending hashtags to get larger reach to people.
- Every member is to start re-tweeting one hour after the original tweet
- This campaign is to happen within the hour of 9am and 6pm respectively every day.

- Track your campaign performance by using the unique campaign hashtag.

14. SPOON FEEDING IDEA

I remember while working with my superior, he always made mention of a particular statement every day before setting out for our daily activities, which I had practiced and worked like magic. He said, and I quote, "For you to have a loyal customer, you have to nurture and spoon feed your existing customers like a baby, you don't just give them food to eat, you feed them with your spoon in a caring manner". The spoon feeding is Pampering. Please pamper your customer. It works like magic.

How to pamper your customer

1) Learn to send SMS messages

2) Put a call through to your customers once in a while

3) When you see a post made by your customer on social media, kindly engage it and drop sweet words.

4) Keep records of your client's personal information such as birthdays so you get to know when their special day is and give a shout out.

5) Appreciate your audience publicly after they have bought your product.

Let us look into our first case study

16. WHATSAPP

Did you know there were over 2 billion active users on WhatsApp as of June 2020, over 1 million new users registering daily, with over 65 billion messages sent out daily in over 180 countries? As a business owner that wants sales upon sales, it is important we use our time and resources on platforms where we have our target audience. Spending our time where there is an active user is more important as our time is money.

As of today, WhatsApp has given businesses much reason to use their powerful business tool for marketing and sales. The rise of WhatsApp product marketing has increased drastically.

However, many are still not exploring this platform as an opportunity to shoot their business to the next level. WhatsApp marketing goes beyond posting your entire product on WhatsApp all at once. If you really want to get active feedback from your ads you will need to come up with creative ways to tell a story about your business. I bet by the time you finish reading this guide you'll be glad you made this decision.

"WhatsApp can only function with contact saved at both ends, to make sales on WhatsApp, the numbers of contacts you have is a huge determinant, but the big question now is who are the calibre of people you saved

their numbers? Are they who can afford your product? Are you selling what they can afford?"

Setting up WhatsApp the right way for marketing and sales

This is the systematic arrangement of your platform to make it easier to use and also bring about more drive to sales. When you set up your platform in an appealing way, you tend to interact conveniently, gaining the ability to surf from one page to another without confusion. Below are the simple ways to set up your platform.

1) Create broadcast lists according to preference:

I will explain what I mean by preference. From your contacts you know who your target audiences are; you do not expect a man to pay attention to your content when what you sell is ladies' products.

Create a broadcast list based on preference. Everybody on your list cannot be your prospect, but you can go through the process of selection and profiling based on their gender, location, age etc.

> *"The same way you select preferences of your audience when you run paid ads is the same way you should focus on saving contacts on WhatsApp"*

Another thing is selling what you cannot afford, your kind of person can say a lot about the kind of contact list you have. If you cannot afford what you sell, 75% of your contacts cannot afford it too. A poor man trying to survive cannot have contacts of rich people saved on his phone (note the phrase rich people) this is not a curse, your cycle and the kind of contacts saved can be a huge determinant.

2) Send short broadcast messages with photos:

This is the fastest way to reach your list with just one click or one message, the conversion rate here is relatively high but that is if you do it the right way.

If you do it wrongly you stand the risk of being muted or blocked, so anything you are doing on this application, always do it in a way you will not feel upset about it.

Posting a large chunk of message to your audience can be so annoying, boring and can also be regarded as spamming. Post your content or product with the right photos and brief message that could involve giving a yes or no response.

Please note that this does not mean you should spam your customers with WhatsApp broadcast messages; ideally you should use WhatsApp to connect with existing loyal customers rather than trying to reach new users. Almost everyone hates messages coming from unknown numbers. If you considered it closely, you'd find that you hate it too.

3) Build customer Loyalty list

Building a customer loyalty list is very important to any business. You have to maintain a customer loyalty list in order to continue the business relationship, this helps you to keep up with your customers/buyers and promote customer loyalty.

Once in a while you can send your loyal customers a shout out or gift items; all these helps motivate them to spread the good news of your product through word of mouth and also give more reasons as to why they should remain loyal to your brand.

4) Learn to send direct message (DM)

People tend to respond to a direct message faster than a broadcast message. Create relationships using DM conversation.

5) When you ask more of questions, you tend to know what your prospects want

Question asking is a very important aspect of marketing; this helps you to know what your prospect is thinking and helps you to create a resolution around the response.

Sometimes who you approach to pitch your product might not be in a good mood to talk to anybody, so how do you get to know this person's mind without blowing your chance up with him, the best way is to ask a simple question like this,

Hello, good day sir, if you do not mind sir, is this a good time to talk to you?

Asking this kind of question will definitely give an answer to your speculation.

What and what not to do on your WhatsApp status.

A) Do not overload your status with images and videos of your products.

As weird as this statement sounds, it is one thing that makes you lose viewers. I know you are trying to make people see your entire content but as much as you are thinking of your brand, think of your consumers too. You don't want them to mute you right? Here is what to do.

-Timing: Everyone hates loads of Images piling up, aside from the fact that a lot of data would go for it, they get bored half way or when it does not load up on time they just tap out. If this keeps happening you might end up being blocked.

Set a time for posting, post 3 times daily. Post just two to three images in the morning as early as 5am, this is the time people get up for their daily activities, they want to see something to start their day, so do not bore them already with loads of images, don't make it too much.

Secondly post 3 more images around 1pm to 2pm, this is the time to go for lunch while at work, then finally post by 5pm. This last phase has high chances of attracting buyers because the day is already out and everyone just wants to relax and see what is going on.

B) Compliment people's status, especially when they are your A list customer, remember customer retention is key. As you expect them to view and respond to your posts, you should do the same.

So, I have been thinking loud on why 90% WhatsApp vendors don't include prices on their products, I had to run a survey to know why. You want to know why?

Well they didn't have any reason, some even said; so they can have a negotiation with them before arriving at a price.

Selling online does not work like that; check top product pages, they always have their prices on it. Online community is where you can make decision if you are buying or not, considering your financial strength.

Always include prices on the items you post, if it is negotiable open a bracket (negotiable). A lot of us have a need of your item but scared to enter your DM to ask for price and eventually not buying because we can't afford it.

This is online marketing not Oyingbo market... The

competition is just too much that someone will enter a vendor's DM to still be asking for price (save your prospect the stress)...LOL The only reason why I will enter

your DM to ask for price is if we are close; because I am sure when I don't eventually buy you won't get upset.

"On the part of the buyer, most vendor always feel you just want to play with them and leave when you don't eventually buy, but in the real sense it is so embarrassing asking for prices and don't buy"

The Free training approach...

Another way to sell on WhatsApp is to make an advert with a landing link to your WhatsApp on how to solve a problem. Let us take a skin care seller as our example.

You are a skin care vendor and you feel the need to expand your client base and make more sales, this is what you should do.

Let's take face pimples as a problem you want to solve, make campaign on a free course to get rid of face pimples.

Anyone that clicks on the link to join your training is your target audience, set a rule that to join the group for the free training, such person must repost your group link (people obviously love free things).

Revealing the step by step approach to solve it the problem, remember this is just a solution out of the several solutions you have being a skin care expert.

Create your group in batches; WhatsApp can only take 256 participants at a time. Whenever you are training your audience on the steps, set the page to only allow the admin to talk then open when you are done.

Make sure to provide answers to their problems, at this point they are getting comfortable with you and feel the need to know other solutions,

You can then introduce other courses or product to them at a cost, create another group chat for these set of people. When you have these people make sure to go in-depth and extra with them as they want to see something new from the previous group.

Sales are guaranteed.

17. TWITTER

Twitter is also another powerful website to make massive sales but this site has been underrated for years with strong competition being rolled out by Facebook and Instagram.

With African countries being below the 20th country using twitter, what does that mean to you? That simply means the world of twitter for business opportunities in Africa has not been fully explored unlike other social media which seems to be saturated with loads of competitions especially instagram.

"Twitter is a great community to interact with people of different race and gender, but have you wondered why

celebrities and "A" list people do not follow you when you follow them. Well, the reason is simple; they do not want their timeline spammed by your content. These people value their time and the contents they are exposed to. On many occasion has many verified badges users followed me. I simply check what I tweet before I tweet or help someone retweet. Twitter, WhatsApp and instagram except Facebook is an end to end thing interface whereby you can only see contents of both parties only when you follow each other. So next time you see an A list person not following you, do not be angry just try to understand them and work on the kind of contents you post"

Twitter seems a bit complicated if you have not created time to love it. To operate efficiently on twitter, you have to love the website and play more with the site.

How to create a standard Twitter account

1) Download the twitter app from play store or apple iOS

2) Complete the form by entering all required information, your email and password

3) Click on create account then next,

4) create a captivating but simple timeline, bio,

5) Proceed to your email to confirm email

6) You are all set up.

7) Upload a clear profile photo and background image

Things not to do on twitter

Avoid spamming by following random people you do not know. An Algorithm has been set on twitter to detect your location and also the location of those you are following. The whole idea about social media is for you to follow those you know, like we have it on Facebook.

Listen carefully as this is very important...

When you follow who you do not know you are at risk of being suspended. So, in case you want to get involved in a follow train, which I believe is not the best choice because the chances of you being blocked are high, it is advisable that you perish that idea. Also, you do not get to interact with your target audience directly because of the randomness. Remember all we preach here is relationship and consistency.

.

Please note that adding or following someone from an unknown location is called spamming.

Below are continuations of what not to do.

1) Do not tweet every second of the day; when you tweet too much twitter regards it as spamming.

2)Do not abuse Hashtags; Hashtags are a way of reaching those that are not on our followers list. Using Hashtags not similar to your content can be regarded as spamming, so only use Hashtags related to your content.

3) Do not tweet once in a month; when you tweet once in a month, you tend to lose followers. A lot of people always try to adjust or balance their following list; they sort it out based on those that have not been active.

4) Do not post long tweets; Research has shown that most times longer tweets do not get engagement unlike a short tweet. Make your tweets brief and well explanatory. Long tweets are mostly boring. If you must make a long tweet, use the thread option, but make sure it connects.

Simple cold ways to hunt for prospects on Twitter

i) Click on the search icon on twitter
ii) Search by key words of what you offer
iii) For example, I offer marketing tips for SME so I am going to search by using this keyword i.e. a keyword based on who my target audience are "accessories"

iv) When "accessories" pops up, look at your upper right-hand side for a two-line nod filter icon, click on it, select anyone of options, and then click near you as the location. It automatically brings post of those talking about that keyword then you can send them a message.

"Another way to hunt prospect is to go to the trending page and send that message. Twitter users on trending are most likely to be online; this is similar to cold calling in outbound marketing to apply in social media marketing, because you do not know these prospects from anywhere but this is an opportunity to shoot your shot"

So, what are you waiting for? I know twitter seems boring to you but those that will increase your customer base portfolio and increase your revenue are waiting for you there, brace yourself and prepare for the task ahead.

18. INSTAGRAM

Instagram was originally launched in 2010 as a check-in application, and then changed into a photo sharing application.

Instagram is non-arguably one of the apex social media platforms after Facebook with a massive rate of influencer and brands on Instagram.

This has quickly turned this website to a fast-growing social ecommerce platform to trade in 2020. In 2019 alone, this website had a whopping 1 billion active users every day.

"Users spend nothing less than 20minuites on the gram. 33% of most stories on Instagram are from businesses. This is to tell you that social media in Nigeria is yet untapped. This is why you have to leverage social media"

This is a virtual platform that relies more on both text and pictures; the aim is for users to share images and videos with their audience.

Plan your Instagram journey and give your brand that face it needs to be known. If you want to stand out on Instagram, then don't post that blurry pictures and vague content.

Setting up an Instagram account

This is quite simple and straight forward but technical when it comes to creating a business account. All you have to do is download the app on play store for android users and on Apple store for IOS users. Set up with a username, email address and password, and when you gain access you then proceed to composing a catchy bio, choosing a profile picture and you are good to go.

The most complex task in this aspect is the Bio setup. You have to do a brief but precise bio that talks about what you do, and how the things you do can solve people's problem, also include good contact information i.e. your contact phone number, email address carrying the name of your company, and also an office address. All these make any visitor trust your brand more.

"Instagram is a highly competitive platform so if you must join, you must be ready for the task ahead"

How to hunt for prospect on Instagram

The easiest way to hunt for customers on Instagram is to create a sales funnel through the usage of sponsored ads to reach larger audience. Create a converting content about your product, introducing a mouth-watering offer that compels them to register with your business with the intension of converting them immediately or later.

But in a case where you have limited resources and you have the need of building customer listing; you will have to work for every customer you add to your portfolio.

Instagram is a bit different from other social media so I use a different approach to hunt. What I do is simple; hunt based on popular celebrities.

Go to the comment section of celebrities; reach out to people commenting to the post using our message template, request to engage with them. Be positive in your approach by leaving a nice message for your prospect either on the comment section or sending a direct message , let your message reflect your intension and be clear about it, it is either they respond back or they don't but trust me, if they respond back you have indeed established a relationship.

(**P.S** the best way to convert on this app is either to run a sponsored post or create an exceptional lead magnet)

19. FACEBOOK

No doubt Facebook is the most sought-after social media platform on earth right now, with new updates about products and offers every day. With over $70 billion dollars as revenue in 2019, that is a huge platform with massive active users.

Have you thought of using the Facebook model to run your business or you are still seeing Facebook as a mere social media platform to interact with friends and family? That's cool as well, but it is about time you start using this website to optimize your sales through the proper usage of Facebook.

How to set up a Facebook page

So, in case you have an existing Facebook account, you do not have to open a new one. All you need to do is go to your Facebook home page,

i)   click on the flag icon
ii)   click on create column and
iii) fill in all the necessary information about your brand
iv)   Viola! You are good to go.

- Next step is to send requests to your Facebook friends from your business page to follow your page. It comes up in the form of an invite.

Do not stop at the invite stage because most of these users have gotten a whole lot of spam as invite to pages, to stand out. you have to chat people up one after the other to join your page with your page link. Yes, it takes a whole lot of stress, but it is worth it.

-After set up, make your first post. Remember you created the page to promote your product so anything you post on the page must be something about your product that people can relate to, be interactive as much as possible. Always seek for your follower's opinion on every of your posts in the form of Questions and anticipate a response.

-Where you have a question being asked by a prospect on your page and you know you cannot provide an immediate answer, be polite to make the follower understand that you will provide information as soon as you get it. All questions about your product must be answered.

Simple ways to hunt for prospects on Facebook

Be consistent when post and do more of question post or relatable post. Facebook and its amazing users, I am 99% sure they engage content when it requires them airing their opinion unlike twitter that swipe off…LOL. Build

relation first before giving offers. Another option is sponsored ads but you know this book is not about that, but you know what, we can teach that on my next edition.

Another organic method you can use...

The search tool, search for a key word

i) Click on the search icon on Facebook

ii) Search by key words of what you offer

iii) For example, I offer marketing tips for SMEs so I am going to search by using this keyword i.e. a keyword based on who my target audience are "accessories"

iv) When "accessories" pops up, it automatically brings post of those talking about that keyword then you can send them a message.

Viola! You have your target audience, send a message.

20.MEASURING IMPRESSION ON SOCIAL MEDIA

This is the parameter used in checking the numbers of views your advert, post or tweet made. Basically, advertising is not for you to purchase a product immediately, it is for you to remember the advertised product when you need the product.

To know your progress or how well content is doing you have to keep a tab on analytics to keep checking your impression.

This can be checked by looking below tweets or posts made by you and click on view activities, this is where you get your impression.

Let us interact on a quick case study; take Indomie Noodles for example Dufil Foods advertises Indomie Noodles every day. What they are trying to do is to send a reminder to you and make it a part of you.

Quote me if I am wrong, while it is not every time you see an Indomie Noodles advert that you purchase Indomie Noodles to eat, but the fastest food you can think of when you are hungry is Indomie Noodles, even without seeing an advert.

They had created an impression that when you are hungry the fastest food you can cook is Indomie Noodles and they follow up with persuasive, emotional and educative adverts, it is simple logic. The impression is calculated on every viewer that views the Ads.

BEST WAYS TO MAKE SALES ON SOCIAL MEDIA

1. Be clear on your objectives and know which type of audience is right for your brand, know who your targets audiences are. Be specific.

2. Understand the audience you are targeting and ensure there is a fit with your own brand.

3. Invest in building long-term relationships with the right audience because relationships will be what will pilot your business when you possibly run out of content.

4. Get the content right and work with audience based on their wants by trying to identify what they want and how they want it and be a good Listener.

5. Do everything in your power to maintain the brand authenticity. Making single authentic sales in a day is better than selling 100 counterfeit products. Sell value always.

6. Be Consistent in whatever you do to promote your brand, when you notice an approach is not bringing in good results, do not hesitate to switch to another approach.

7. You need to deliver the right message to the right audience at the right time.

Having your goals outlined makes it easier to give your audience what they want and also makes it easier for you as a brand owner to know where your weakness lies and where you have your strength.

8. Ensure you measure your results as you proceed with making your product known to your audience, never stop testing and measuring.

WHEN IS THE APPROPRIATE TIME TO POST ON SOCIAL MEDIA

There is no specific time to post content on social media, it all boils down to knowing the right time to post. This is very essential to know because it can also decide your conversion rate. We all want to have content where everyone can engage and in turn maybe close a deal or profile a prospect.

If you are not posting content at the right time the likelihood of you getting an impressive response will be relatively low, no one wants that as far as business is concerned. You might be spending the right amount of time, energy, and resources on a brand and still be getting the wrong signal.

This happens when the right thing is being done wrongly. To curb this inappropriate act, we have to learn to understand our audience first.

Understanding your audience

A thing to give much attention to on social media is timing. Try to identify your audience and also know when your target audiences are always online. Those audiences who work 9-5 are most likely to be active online very early in the morning and in the evening as they would want to know what is happening on the internet before starting their daily activities and also at the end of the day when they are through with work.

Timing is an indicator to always observe before posting on social media, each industry timing differs so it is left to you to observe and document when your audience is active. Use your analytics to determine the demographics of your followers and when the best time to post is.

"Above all, you want to post when you will have time to engage with your followers who comment on your posts. A good rule is to be engaging for about 20 minutes before your post and continue engaging for 30 minutes after, this way your audience knows you are active and they are ready to engage"

SOCIAL MEDIA INDICATORS

Before the digital age, to calculate performance was way too strenuous and require more man power, resources and time. But digital marketing has solved that gap and things have changed drastically now, the insights on posts will let you calculate your progress. These can also be referred to as key performance indicators.

"Key performance indicators are distinctive numerical metrics that are used to track or measure the

performance or progress of a defined goal or campaigns. These indicators play a very crucial role when it comes to posting and campaigns"

Previously we have discussed what it means to understand who our audiences are, right? Now we look at the parameters that are regarded as indicators which can be used to measure our audience attitude and response to posts, also how we can utilize these indicators to generate sales. We will be mentioning a few of the countless variables to measure performance of post content.

TOP LOCATION

This is the statistical analysis of top players in post engagement by their location. This is an important indicator in the measurement of performance as it makes you understand where most of your prospects are engaging from.

For example: you made a post of a concert coming up in Kampala, when you check your post analysis you see that most of your audiences are from Lagos Nigeria. What this simply means is that since you are getting more response from Nigeria, then you should be ready for more Nigerians at your events. Remember, this is about posting without sponsored ads so you do not have the power to select the location of your audience.

Posting and targeting location without sponsored ads can only be achieved with the use of keywords, hashtags trending in a particular location; also shout out help from friends in the same region to target people within the desired location.

Also, you can use a worldwide trending hashtag to access a general trend, I call this organic campaign unlike sponsored ads which is Bot influenced.

"Sponsored ads are good no doubt but it is important you know how to create them; also, it involves a lot of money to operate. When you spend a fortune on sponsored ads then you must be getting it right. Everyone's dream is to have a more realistic and engaging campaign that will drive traffic then sales"

GENDER

Gender metrics is the sex of your audience [male or female]. This is another indicator to look out for as it will tell you the sex of those engaging in your post. Our opinions towards things can be different based on gender, we all might come to a conclusion that men love cars and sports while women love shopping and reality shows.

This can also mean a lot on the product that you introduce to people; the simple example stated earlier might have reflected our reality. Behavioural and psychological differences between men and women are centred on gender studies. Many advertisers now focus their techniques around gender tailoring advertising content to target men or women.

"In our early days growing up, we all must agree that the behavioural patterns of both sexes are different and it is by default to say that girls would opt for playing with stuffed animals and dolls while boys would opt for toy cars and balls. The toy industry has leveraged on this for years creating the needs of both genders separately and making a huge profit out of the toy industry"

Now even in adulthood, this gender metrics is still being used by companies to target their audience, for example the perfume and fragrance industry. They make perfumes based on gender as female perfumes would be more of a floral and sweet light scent while male perfumes come in strong with a touch of smoky or woody fragrance.

Even Victoria's Secret was targeted at women; from the name have we ever asked if truly Victoria has a secret? Or the secret is being tightened in a bottle just like a genie? Whatever the case may be, the brand is centred on female lingerie, which is highly evident in the name.

All these are target marketing based on gender.

Gender is an indicator we should always consider when making our marketing decisions. We all must agree that the shopping pattern for men and women is quite different as men would go a straight way to getting his choice of product on a shelf and leave, while women would walk the whole store comparing prices to product, as it is female nature to get the perfect solution to their problem.

Even if they get a product that would solve their problem, they still would not go for the product immediately as pricing might be another problem.

"A woman's decision-making process is more complex and lengthier than that of men. So, if you put a product out there, maybe by putting out a survey to get your statistics right, be cautious of who your target audience are and how you can satisfy their needs accordingly"

Examples of what men would want and what women would prefer

-Men would want bigger cars for enjoyment while women would prefer smaller cars with focus on functionality.
-Men would want electronic and technological gadgets while women would prefer consumer electronics.

-Men would want shaving powder and foam while women would prefer cosmetics, perfumes and deodorants.
-Men would want to have beer and spirits while women would prefer to have wine, champagne and soft drinks.

- Men would want to watch football and play bets while women would prefer watching soap operas and spend on makeup.

When you know for sure what your audience wants by gender then you can know how to satisfy them by developing different strategy for different gender.

FOLLOWERS

Followers are the users that support a person or a particular set of ideas. Having so many followers does not guarantee that any post by you will be engaged; a lot of attribute might influence the non engagement of content, these ranges from;

- suspended accounts of followers
- loss of login details
- loss of logged in gadget
- inactive accounts
- Ghost followers/users
- Hacked accounts and many more

All these might be some of the few reasons why you are not having engagement on your contents. People live with different perception and beliefs; a large number of individuals believes your engagement all depends on the numbers of followers you have i.e. the higher the numbers of followers you have the higher the number of engagement; while few individuals believes that the numbers of followers you have do not influence your engagement.

Well, I will agree with the few people that believe that the numbers of followers do not determine your engagement and conversion rate. [See explanation under influencing marketing]

"The diagram above describes the statistical analytics of when your followers are most active to engage your post.
It is not a new thing that the most active and engaging days are the weekend. These are the days in which most people are free and just want to know what is happening on the internet and also socialize with family and friends"

Age Range

This is one of the indicators to be considered before targeting your campaign. In an automated campaign this is very easy as you are to give a Bot an instruction by selecting an algorithm to which it will function on. Well do not forget this is an article on how to run campaigns and make sales without sponsored ads.

This can be very hard to determine who your prospective audience could be as this kind of campaign is more likely to seen by different age group.

This can only be achieved by testing and checking your analytics on every campaign to determine who are the highest viewers or engagers of your content.

Seeing post insight helps to know how to construct your post i.e. putting experience in consideration according to age, have background knowledge about prospects and clients; help create a market based on age insight. Content can be structured knowing that there are different users with their opinion and age, belief and understanding.

25. HASHTAGS

Hashtags are unique keywords that are preceded by a hash sign which are basically used to identify a topic, word or campaign. People most times search by hashtags to get every information about a particular campaign.

On Twitter for example, trending is almost like a community where everyone visits to share and discuss opinions on a certain topic. 70 percent of twitter users visit trending at least once in a day and every other social media uses hashtags to track a post; if anyone knows what the hashtag about a topic is, they can easily search using the hashtag and get the information they required.

"Why twitter seems more concerned about hashtags is because twitter is more like an instant interactive inter-phase where new tweets automatically push previous tweets down the timeline which makes it very easy for anyone to miss information which has been previously shared by a user. That is why a retweet icon was put in place to re-establish the tweets that has been previously tweeted; and also, to make sure everybody can be a part of the conversation"

I must say, twitter is the most interactive platform for people from different cultural backgrounds. This is the kind of platform you should leverage your business on and make sales.

Hashtags makes people find what they seek online mainly by clicking or search with the hashtags. When I feel a need to search for contents about digital marketing, I simply search by the hashtag *#digitalmarketing*and all available information about digital marketing only files out, so this saves the stress of getting distracted with other content.

On some social media platforms like Instagram, you are allowed to use up to 30 hashtags to market your product but trust me when you have something outside your hashtags not relating to your content, Instagram automatically knows, and your account might get penalized for that. Therefore, whatever you may be posting ensure to use the right hashtags that will bring in your type of audience. If you are a cloth vendor all the hashtags to use should be around clothing and clothing alone.

"A lot of us are fond of bringing in celebrities' names on our hashtags, this is pretty bad. When making hashtags, think of a hashtag that you are sure people can search with and related to your business. Avoid using Hashtags with more than 300,000 posts, your content might get lost instead use hashtags with 1000 posts"

WAYS TO BUILD YOUR BRAND ORGANICALLY

There are loads of ways to build your brand organically without abusing the hashtags. To mention a few

-Stay consistent

For every business that has a vision for long term, they must learn to be consistent in whatever they do. Staying consistent is the hardest thing to do, it will get to a point where you might run out of the content or the zeal to keep posting and engaging is not there anymore. That is the time you have to motivate yourself that giving up is never an option.

Consistency is key to everything. You might meet a prospect today that does not need to buy your product now but as time goes on with the right communication strategy and being consistent with reaching out and treating such prospect just like you are treating your client, such a prospect will learn to know your brand and might even see your brand as a choice later.

"Indomie is a brand that has been in existence in West Africa for decades now and is still waxing stronger. They have been able to stay this long even with the strong competition going on because they are consistent. A lot of noodles manufacturing companies that came after have already winded up. Stay consistent, stay focused"

-Engage peoples post

It is never a bad idea to engage a prospect's post first. By engaging their post, it shows you place them on high esteem and the prospect will feel honoured and recognized.

Such person would see you are very down to earth and if there is any need to get your product, I am sure such person would get in touch. One big secret about engaging first is that it gives the ground for conversation, most times when I engage a prospect's post, I engage not because I cannot ignore the post but because I want to get in a conversation with such a prospect.

I know of a lady on twitter that kept posting tweets every day without getting any engagements. I knew she was very active on twitter but the reason why she was not getting engagements was because she kept tweeting without aim, she tweeted everything that came to her head.

Well, I engaged one of her tweets and the next thing I saw was a direct message asking me to teach her how to have an engaging tweet. I taught her the tricks just like I engaged her tweets; she started engaging people's tweets and eventually they started reciprocating. That is how you grow; it is tit for tat, one step at a time.

-Upload amazing photos and high-quality videos

Social media is a community where we have a lot of competitors that will not mind to knock you off just to have their brand known. One of the best ways to stay relevant in the industry is to be consistent with the posting of high-quality photos and videos. Research has it that posts with quality photos and videos convert more prospects to clients than posts with low quality photos and videos. People tend to interact more with pictures with good quality.

-Share testimonies and reviews on your story

When you have a review from a customer, always post them on your story and feeds, the nature of man is centred on learning from one another; most people will trust and may patronize your brand because of a review being posted. When I see a review about a product, I assume the product has been used by someone and give good feedback.

-Set a target of ten engagements every day

This is a very important parameter that must be noted, without sponsored ads you have to learn to engage people's posts to get feedback. I set a schedule for myself to always engage 5 targets everyday then as time went by, I increased it to 10 targets. To build a sustainable brand you have to learn how to hunt clients and close deals with them.

- Motivational quotes card on events and anniversary, FAQ frequently asked questions

Share more motivational quotes on anniversary and events, things people can relate to, and post infographics pictures on frequently asked questions. A FAQ is a self-service question being asked to answer questions asked by prospects and customers.

-Search for vendors selling your kind of product and look out for the hashtags they use (Copycat Approach)

This is one thing every small-scale business owner should take note, to grow your business; you have to look out for bigger businesses in the same line of business with you. Take a good study of how they operate and how they post contents online. This will take a while to study but it will be worth it.

"Most of these top brands buy high converting keywords and hashtags, if you leverage on this you might be hitting a jackpot. In everything one must do to grow you should have a guide or mentor; make top brands your mentor so one day you can be like them or even higher"

-Ask for shout outs from family and friends

This has been the most effective and fastest way to convert and to make your brand known organically. Share your content with pictures and also a link to land on your page for conversion with friends and family members. Ask your family members to vouch and write a review on your behalf.

When you share your content with them for reposts, endeavour to always send a reminder to them to know if any question is asked by any of their contacts, if any questions arises, kindly request for the prospect contact number and engage to convert.

- Attend Events and community programs to share your page and handle to people.

When you attend events, learn to go with two orientations; represent your brand and also go for whatever you are invited for. Share your social media handle with random prospects and introduce your brand, do not forget it is a social gathering.

-Have an everyday target.

Rome was not built in a day so we have to keep working to build our brand, set an everyday target and make sure you meet up with the target every day.

In fact, I have a chat of operations all set on a timer, so if by chance I forget to perform one task, the timer triggers my attention.

REVIEWS AND RATINGS

Research has it that 52 percent of consumers search online and/or check the business web site to check for reviews before buying or before visiting a new business.

Also, Customer review influences more than 86 percent of online customers but the weirdest truth about reviews and rating is that most brands go as far as getting fake reviews on their page or website to get the attention of visitors.

This is a very bad idea for brand that has a vision for sustainability, because as soon as this secret is leaked; the whole reputation of the brand gets compromised. I mean no secret can remain secret forever so why not focus on growing your business slowly and steady rather than seeking a short and faster means that leads to nowhere.

I remembered vividly a trend about a cosmetic vendor on twitter, she shared a screenshot of her reviews; unknowingly to her, she had wrongly uploaded image carrying the name of her other cell phone line (she was sending review from her two lines, then crop out the names to show her audiences.) please do not join this trail, one original review is better than loads of deceits and lies.

"Reviews are very important component of building a credible brand"

Rating and reviews work together but they are different, reviews are just a feedback interpreted in written text while ratings are mostly inform of scales of 1 to 5. Some ratings come with space to write a short text feedback. All these helps brand to know where they are lagging behind as well as to know their best-selling product.

This can be used to measure product strength in an organisation, companies leverage on this to serve their customers well.

Some examples application that uses reviews and ratings are our social media pages, the pop-up notification after using a new application for a while, that's reviews and rating pops, Amazon, Google play stores amongst others, you can also use it for your business.

So, to grow your business keeping your brand reputation in mind, kindly do the following.

- Politely ask for reviews from your customer

-Reply your customer reviews on public pages privately to avoid public opinion dispute

- Prioritize responding to reviews, this shows how much you care.

OFFLINE MARKETING

Offline marketing is any advertising that is carried out with the use of old means of marketing as opposed this new age marketing i.e. traditional marketing. It is also a means of advertisement which includes billboards, televisions, radios etc. Offline marketing as it implies does not need the use of internet to carry out a campaign.

As much as online marketing is the aim of every brand in this 21stcentury, offline marketing cannot be pushed aside. As much as we have our online presence active, our offline presence should not be deleted from the plan.

That is why you see that big organisations despite millions of dollars on their online presence, they still make their offline available. Depending solely on online presence is not advisable.

This is a well-tested approach to build brand awareness, test new regional markets, and build offline marketing in an online conversion. Below are few ways of reaching audience in an offline approach.

1) **Word of mouth:** Word of mouth remains one of the easiest and cheapest ways of marketing. This involves people talking about your brand or product positively from person to person. This can only be achieved if you have a good product that gives you good reputation out there. Also, you can

partner with friends who have similar products as you for deals and offers.

Word of mouth happens when a customer experiences something far beyond what is expected. Check out if you have a small business group in your area where you can join, attend meetings, and hangout to discuss more on how you can grow your business.

As fast as word of mouth can build your brand, the same way it can destroy it. Let me explain.

I always preach value to every business owners and sales representative I have come in contact with; the logic is simple, it is better customers speak well of your product to people or not speak of it at all, than to speak badly of brand. Positive feedback is what everyone wishes for; customer centric experience is the goal.

2) **Business cards:** This is also a nice way to market your product too, design a meaningful precise card that solves a problem. No one likes a boring and busy business card. Most times when creating a business card, always include a phrase that asks questions somewhere at the back of the card. Something like: "Do you have a question to ask or an inquiry to make?" would suffice, and then include your contact details right below the question tag. This way people know you can solve their problems, this is a simple tactic I believe everyone should adopt.

"The human brain is designed to respond to stimuli, subconsciously seeing the question tag behind the card, they would respond. Share your business cards at events, family gatherings, and even to a new friend on the street"

3) Banners:Posters and banners do not cost much to make. These can be printed and showcased at your place of business.

This is a proven approach to sales especially to a start-up business. Have you asked yourself to how much big organisation spends of big static billboards just like your banner? Why do they invest n that? How has that been able to influence their sale? Well if they have not been getting responses from the content board, they will not be investing heavily in it. For a small-scale enterprise, I advise you make small banners with a call to action (phone numbers, email, social media pages and even your business website if any) boldly written on it, hang in your community and see how this influence your sales. Mostly smaller banners can be hanged anywhere and it is mostly free.

4) Referral:When you have made a good reputation for some customers in the past you can politely ask them for referrals.

This form of making sales is so underrated. Referrals give rest of mind and inculcate trust on the part of the buyer. For instance, my brother purchased a car from a dealer; when it is time to buy my own car, I might probably buy from the dealer because the referral is coming from my brother and I trust him.

5) Billboard: This is a large outdoor board for displaying advertisement to reach much audience within a particular period of time; it could be in digital or static form.

This is one of the oldest forms of advertisements platform which is still in trend today. Impression on a bill board is being calculated by the calculating the numbers of people that were able to see the advert.

Previous years before technological advancements, impression were calculated by estimating the numbers of people that passes through the bill board location at that given; time but now, artificial intelligence AI has replaced the estimation of man; a billboard AI can easily track the numbers of mobile devices of passer by thereby giving the accurate numbers of people that might have seen the billboard advert for that particular day. Isn't that amazing!

UNDERSTANDING TRAFFIC ON YOUR SOCIAL PAGES AND WEBSITES

In layman understanding, this is when you have visitors coming to your page. Traffic on your page could mean an increase in sales. We have to understand how to drive converting traffic, not just mere visitors to our pages and websites. I do not mean traffic on the highway; I am referring to traffic in marketing.

"Traffic in marketing can be regarded as visitors to your website or page and this can be categorized into segments depending on how the visitors found you. Traffics are basically categorized into two which include traffic by human and traffic by bot which can also be referred to as automated traffic"

Bot traffic is a traffic that involves computer programs designed to automatically roam the internet to engage websites and pages while human traffic is the one that involves human engagement to your page or website.

Of course, we all care about traffic by human more to bot programs, automotive bots tend to expose website and pages to compromise which is why it is not always advisable to go for automatic traffics. Let us try to identify where human traffic comes from because that is all we care about at this point in time.

1) Organic traffic: organic traffic is the traffic that comes from search engines as a result of humans trying to look out for products or services online, hence searching by keywords to arrive on your page.

2) Paid traffic: This is the opposite of organic traffic. This involves the use of sponsored ads to generate traffic to your page. For example you create a topic on a product or service and you want it to get across to a wide range of people; then you pay to get the exposure done, hence traffic is redirected to your page or website, and this is usually on a pay per click basis (PPC).

3) Affiliate traffic: This is when you have an affiliate program that you run on page or website, maybe to a product offer or service, any visitor you get as a result of the affiliate program link is referred to as affiliate traffic.

4) Direct traffic: This type of traffic originates as a result of people typing in your website address in a browser to arrive at your page; this is mostly relatively low to the means of traffic as explained earlier.

5) Referral traffic: Referral traffic generates as a result of the referral link being shared by friends and family on their pages or website.

6) Email traffic: This type of traffic generates from the clicks on email messages. I know most of us might have come across loads of unsolicited emails dropping into our email boxes; most of them are targeted to drive traffic to pages and websites. When next you see an email, you might as well want to help someone drive traffic to their page.

7) Social traffic: This involves the sharing of a website or page link on social media pages. When next you see a link on social media, it is a link to drive traffic to a website or a page.

CONCLUSION

Selling can be considered an art form. Like any other art form, it takes time to master and perfect, even with proper guidance. However, with proper guidance, you tend to spend more time on effective techniques than you would have if you go at it alone. With all that has been discussed in this book, the secret to sale is now in the palm of your hands, and you can become a sales powerhouse if all the guidelines are followed fastidiously. Goodluck!

30. GLOSSARY

1) Social media: These are websites and applications that enable users to create and share content or to participate in social networking.

2) Marketing: This is the activity, set of institutions, and processes for creating, communicating, delivering, and exchanging offerings that have value for customers, clients, partners, and society at large.

3) Website: A website is a collection of web pages and related content that is identified by a common domain name and published on at least one web server

4) Traffic: *traffic* is the amount of data sent and received by visitors to a *website or page*

5) Sales: This is a term used to describe the activities that lead to the selling of goods or services

6)   Prospect: a probability or chance for future success, especially as based on present work

7)   Customer: A customer is an individual or business that purchases another company's goods or services.

8)   Client: person who pays a professional person or organization for service

9)   Cold calling: This is a technique in which a salesperson contacts individuals who have not previously expressed interest in the offered products or services

10) Brand: this is an identifying symbol, mark, logo, name, word, and/or sentence that companies use to distinguish their product from others.

11) Infographics: This is a representation of information in a graphic format designed to make the data easily understandable at a glance.

12) Leads: sales lead is a person or business who may eventually become a client. Sales lead also refers to the data that identifies an entity as a potential buyer of a product or service.

13) Strategy: This is a plan or set of plans set to achieve something.

14) Advertisement: This is how a company encourages people to buy their products and services or ideas with different strategies and means.

15) Digital marketing: this is a branch of marketing that make use of internet based digital technologies such as computers, cell phones and other digital platforms to promote products and services

16) Search engines: search engine is a web-based tool that enables users to locate information on the World Wide Web (WWW)

17) Content marketing: this a type of marketing that involves the creation and sharing of online material (such as videos, blogs, and social media posts) that does not explicitly promote a brand but is intended to stimulate interest in its products or services

18) Sponsored ads: This is a type of advertising where a company pays to be associated with a specific event

19) Packaging: This can be referred to the wrapping or bottling of products to make them safe from damages and also to give them a unique look to differentiate them from the regular relative product.

20) Public policy: This is the process by which governments translate their political vision into programs and actions to deliver outcomes

21) Subscription: This is to give consent or approval or to arrange to receive something, typically a publication, regularly by paying in advance.

22) Customer experience: this is the holistic perception of their *experience*with your business or brand.

23) Loyal customer: This is when a person transacts with a brand on an ongoing basis for a period of time.

24) Competitive: This is relating to or characterized by competition; or when a group of people or brands are trying to win a contest.

25) Impression: Impressions are not action-based and are merely defined by a user potentially seeing the

advertisement, this is the numbers of times a prospect sees an advert or post on a media platform.

26) **Customer service:** this is the process of providing timely, attentive, top notch service to a customer, and making sure their needs are met as soon as possible.

27) **Feedback:** This is the information about reactions to a product; a person's performance of a task in marketing is regarded to as Customer feedback

28) **Media:** These are communication outlets or tools used to store and deliver information or data.

29) **Conversion:** this is the process of changing or causing something to change from one form to another.

30) **Promotional:** This is the process of publicizing a product or service so as to increase sales or public awareness

.

31) Index: This is an indicator or measure of something. This could be in statistical or alphabetical measure.

32) Performance: This is the completion of a task with application of knowledge, skills and abilities.

33) Service: This is an intangible product and it involves the process of getting things done for someone or the action of helping or doing work for someone

34) Audience: These are your target prospects; they are assembled spectators or listeners ready to consume your product or service.

35) Complaint: This is an unsatisfactory or unacceptable statement about something maybe product and service sometimes.

.

36) Educational: This is relating to education. In marketing this is the process of putting out educative content out to the public

37) Story telling: This is the process of making a connection with the customer selling a product through telling a real story well.

38) Investor: This is an individual, company or entity that invests capital with the aim of making a profit.

39) Data: This is the information gathered about the demand for goods, such as the number of units sold, and the value of goods sold.

40) Persuasion: This is the use of psychological techniques to manipulate how customers feel towards your product or service i.e. it is art of using the way humans think to make prospects buy your product.

41) Authority: This is the process of becoming so well known as an expert in your target market such that prospects will look out for our brand.

42) Marketer: This is a person whose duties include the identification of the product and services desired by a set of consumers or users, as well as the *marketing*of those products and services on behalf of a company

43) Psychology: This is the overall feeling among market participants that impels them to buy or sell.

44) Broadcast list: this is the saved lists of message recipients that you can repeatedly send broadcast messages to without having to select them each time.

45) Preference: This is the state of being preferred or liked.

46) Visibility: the state of being able to be seen.

47) Spamming: This is the act of sending the same message indiscriminately to large number of Internet users, or performing same action repeatedly.

48) Pitching: The process of introducing a product or service to a set of individuals or audience.

49) Suspended: This is the act of putting an action or a person on hold, this is always temporary.

50) Comment: This is a written or verbal remark or response to something or the act of responding or expressing opinion.

51) Hashtags: This is a word or phrase preceded by a hash sign; this is typically used on social media to drive a specific topic.

52)   Business: This involves an entity engaged in commercial activities solely for the aim of getting profit.

53) Revenue: This can simply be regarded as profit being generated by an organization or business operation which includes discounts and deductions.

54) Target audience: this is the intended people or reader of an advert or publication, they are predetermined set of consumers an advert or product is aimed at.

55) Authenticity: This is proven fact of legitimacy and original.

56) Counterfeit: This means something that is made to look like original but really is not but fraudulent in nature.

57) Conversion rate: This is the process of causing something to change from one form to another with the help of persuasion techniques.

58) Industry: This can also be referred to a group where we have people with common goal and interest or a clique of same producer of a product or service.

59) Indicator: This is a parameter that indicates the state or level of something.

60) Influence: This is the capacity to have an effect on something or people, the act of using one's capacity to manipulate an action.

61) Campaign: This is a planned set of activities carried out by people for a period of time. This is an action of setting up a product advert on social media.

63) Followers: A follower is a person who admires a particular person or set of idea. Follower on instagram, twitter and Facebook has the same meaning.

64) Consistency: This is the quality of always being the same or behaving or performing in a similar way over a period of time.

65) Decade: This is a period of ten years.

66) Tricks: This is a way of manipulating or a scheme intended to convince someone.

67) Product: This is an item offered for sale,

68) Sustainability: This is the rate at which a brand meets the needs of the present without compromising the ability of future generations to meet their needs.

69) Keywords: These are words that serve as key to the meaning of another word, a sentence, passage, or the likes

70) Reviews: These are comments or opinions after using a product, reviews can either come in good or bad.

71) Organic marketing: This is the act of getting your customers to come to you naturally over time, rather than artificially paid links or boosted post.

72) Affiliate Marketing: This is the process of earning a commission by promoting other people's products.

73) Referral marketing: Itis the method of promoting products or services to new customers through referrals; this usually involves word of mouth.

References:

Inspiration and knowledge are been drawn from the following sources.

1) Alux.com
2) Small business big money by Akin Alabi
3) Google and wikipedia

www.ingramcontent.com/pod-product-compliance
Lightning Source LLC
LaVergne TN
LVHW051332050326
832903LV00031B/3490